Ralph Broome

Letters from Simkin the Second to his Dear Brother in Wales

Containing an Humble Description of the Trial of Warren Hastings, Esq.

Ralph Broome

Letters from Simkin the Second to his Dear Brother in Wales
Containing an Humble Description of the Trial of Warren Hastings, Esq.

ISBN/EAN: 9783744716246

Printed in Europe, USA, Canada, Australia, Japan

Cover: Foto ©ninafisch / pixelio.de

More available books at **www.hansebooks.com**

FROM

SIMPKIN THE SECOND

TO HIS

DEAR BROTHER IN WALES;

CONTAINING AN

HUMBLE DESCRIPTION OF THE TRIAL

OF

WARREN HASTINGS, Esq.

WITH

SIMON's ANSWER.

———————

D U B L I N:

PRINTED FOR P. BYRNE, GRAFTON-STREET,
AND J. MOORE, COLLEGE-GREEN.

———————

M.DCC.LXXXVIII.

FROM

SIMPKIN THE SECOND

TO HIS

DEAR BROTHER IN WALES.

––––––––

With an humble Defcription of the prefent Trial.

––––––––

DEAR BROTHER,

—— THE Letter I formerly fent you,
I hope was defcriptive enough to content you—
With refpeſt to PROCESSION, and *taking of Places*,
My Mafters and Judges, by Lordfhips and Graces:
According to promife, I now fhall defcribe
The Proceffion of BURKE, and his Eloquent Tribe—

Firft,

First, EDMUND walks in at the head of the Groupe,
That powerful Chief of that powerful Troop—
What awful folemnity's feen in his gait,
Whilft the Nod of his Head beats due time to his Feet!
CHARLES FOX is the fecond, and clofe on his right,
Whofe waddle declares he will never go ftraight.
The rubicund SHERIDAN enters the third,
The Oppofer of PITT, and the Treafury Board—
His attention, 'tis faid, has fo long been directed
To the *National Debts*, that his own are neglected—
And in Public Affairs, when fuch management's fhewn,
No wonder a man cannot think of his own.
Next ADAM comes in, with a fpit at his fide,
And ftruts like a Turkey-Cock, fwelling with pride:
Then ANSTRUTHER follows, that Weather-Cock Elf,
Who fhews how a Man may *diffent* from—HIMSELF—
To the *Governor* HASTINGS, his praife was profufe;
On *Prifoner* HASTINGS, he pours forth abufe—
Then follows *Young* GREY, an exact imitator
Of the fcurrilous BURKE, a moft promifing Prater:
Tho' all muft lament that he's under fuch Banners,
" As Evil Community fpoils our Good Manners."
Then PELHAM, FITZPATRICK, and WINDHAM came
    forth,
With MONTAGUE, MAITLAND, with BURGOYNE and
    North.

CHICK

CHICK TAYLOR, and ERSKINE, are join'd in the Vote,
And as MANAGERS known, by—a Bag and dress Coat.
Then FRANCIS comes sneaking, with grief in his heart,
At not being indulg'd with a MANAGER's *part*—
Tho' he now and then steals to the Managers' Box,
To suggest a shrewd Question to BURKE and CHARLES
  FOX.
The COMMONS, from *riding* who have any leisure,
In order come in, and go out at their pleasure—
Now the Court is assembled, in form to begin,   ⎫
And SHERRY begs leave to call *Middleton* in,   ⎬
That name, at whose sound there's a general grin— ⎭
Five days has *Poor* MIDDLETON sweated and stew'd;
Their Questions were artful, his Answers were shrewd—
He was ask'd, " If the *Eunuch* ALMASS *had a Child?*"
Lord THURLOW look'd black, and the Ladies all smil'd;
The Witness made answer, " I really can't say;"
The powers of his Mem'ry were melted away.——
  Q. Have you e'er seen the BEGUMS ?—He answer'd,
   I've not:
  Q. Pray mention their persons?—*A.* Indeed I've forgot.
  Q. What may in Rebellion your principles be,
   Or can you the probable consequence see
   Or Men rising in Arms, and o'er-running the Na-
   tion ?
  He reply'd, " 'Tis a Question of *deep Speculation.*"
          Q. When

Q. When the Eunuchs were fetter'd, pray what did they feel?

Were they thinking of Poifon, the Rack, or the Wheel?

Or what do you think might have been their intentions?

A. I concern not myfelf about their apprehenfions.

Q. How many young damfels were in the *Khord Mhal?*

A. I do not believe I can recollect all.

Q. Say—What were their wifhes, or what was their view?

A. I cannot remember that ever I knew.

Q. When they threaten'd to throw themfelves over the Wall,

What induc'd them to hazard the getting a fall?

A. I do not remember they did fo at all.

Q. What did GORDON addrefs to the *Begum* that Letter?

A. He *himfelf* is in Court, and can anfwer you better.

Q. You were at *Lucknow* in the year Eighty-two?

A. I'm inclin'd to believe what you fay may be true.

Q. Have YOU any doubts of it?——And if fo, *how many?*

A. I believe not; I think I cannot *have any.*

Q. The PRISONER's *Defence;* did you pen part or not?

A. I had fome Converfation with Major JOHN SCOTT.

Q. With

Q. With the *Counfel* of HASTINGS were you at the
     Hall ? *

A. I might *accidentally* give them a call.

Q. What, went accidentally with Major SCOTT ?

A. I really don't know ; if I did, I've forgot.

Q. Do Children in India their Parents efteem ?
     Do they love their *Mammas?* or how ftrong do
       you deem
     Their affection may be ? or, pray can you tell,
     If Papa and Mamma are lov'd equally well ?

A. Some perhaps love their Father, and fome love
     their Mother,
     And fome Children like neither *one* nor the *other.*

Q. Does the Son, by the Laws of the *Koran,* fucceed
     To the Father's Eftate ?—*A.* Yes, the eldeft in-
     deed.

Q. May the Mother that Property legally keep,
     Lodg'd where fhe and her Hufband do ufually fleep?

A. I am rather inclin'd to be led, I confefs,
     To believe that the Wife no fuch right does poffefs.

When SHERRY had finifh'd this Examination,
He their Lordfhips addrefs'd with this florid Oration ;—
" My LORDS ! to your Lordfhips, it needs muft appear,
" That the Charges are founded on evidence clear.

       * Drapers' Hall.

                      " My

" My Lords, pray attend, whilft I fpeak more at large,

" And apply what we've heard to eftablifh the Charge.

" ALMASS *had a Son,* whom the Prifoner deftroy'd;

" The *Begums* were Dames, who rich jointures enjoy'd :

" Large extenfive Jaghires, and for that only reafon,

" The Prifoner declared they were guilty of Treafon.——

" We have prov'd, no Rebellion was ftirr'd up by them,

" And that HASTINGS was not authoris'd to condemn,

" The Eunuchs to fuffer the Rack and the Wheel ;——

" ——For Eunuchs, tho' fuch, *many know,* they can feel——

" That two thoufand Young Damfels lived in the ⎞
  " *Khord Mhal,*   ⎟

" Who threw themfelves headlong juft over the wall, ⎬

" That the SEAPOYS might catch them—and fo break ⎟
 - " their fall ;——   ⎠

" That their views and intentions were but to efcape

" The danger of HASTINGS *committing a Rape;*

" The BEGUMS themfelves, were afraid left his plea-
fures,

" Should extend to their *Perfons,* as well as their *Trea-*
 " *fures*——

" How licentious, how wicked, how bafe are the men,

" Who would ravifh old women of threefcore and ten !

" Oh ! *Great* GOD *of Juftice !* Can'ft thou think it fit-
ting,

" To look down from thy Throne, while fuch Rapes are
 " committing ?

            " Why

" Why delay then to fix fome perpetual mark,

" At once to difable this infamous Spark;

" Who fet off from CALCUTTA, determined to rob

" Some *fat* ZEMINDAR, or fome *wealthy* NABOB.—

" No prey found this Tyger in reach of his fpring,

" Save the BEGUMS *of Oude*, and the *Rajah Cheyt Sing.*

" Like a Robber, whofe choice is reftri&ed to two,

" No place, except *Bagfhot* and *Hounflow*, will do.

" I have prov'd that the Prifoner is *all over guilt;*

" That hogfheads of innocent blood he has fplit;

" I have prov'd he was guilty, of Fraud and Abufe,

" And Robbery too, for the Company's ufe—

" Then by our RELIGION, which he has difgrac'd;

" By our CONSTITUTION, which he has defac'd;

" By Nature's beft rights, I your Lordfhips invoke,

" Thofe rights to *whofe heart he has given a* POKE—

" By the Chaftity pure of the BEGUMS *of Oude;*

" By millions of dead men, now crying aloud;

" Thofe dead men, whofe deaths all to murder were

  " owing,

" Whilft tears from their wives were in rivulets flowing:

" By thofe poor diftreft damfels, who fra&ur'd their

  " bones,

" By haftily throwing their bodies on ftones——

" Ye BISHOPS! ARCHBISHOPS! a fan&ified band!

" Who all holy myfteries well underftand!

     " Ye

" Ye *Judges of England*, of wifdom profound,
" Who can find out the Law, and can lofe it—when
     " found :
" Ye *Nobles*, in ermine, fo fpotlefs a train,
" Whofe Honour can fuffer by no blot or ftain ;
" Ye Royal Young Princes—for Chaftity fam'd,
" For clear underftandings, which need not be nam'd—
" To you, all *Indoftan* looks up for relief,
" And Vengeance demands on that *Robber* and *Thief!*—
" Unlefs by your juftice his blood fhall be fpilt,
" The World will affirm you partake of his guilt ;.
" Shed his blood then, I fay !—No, the *hanging of one*,
" For the *Slaughter of* Millions, can never atone.—
" He ought to be tortur'd with racks, gripes, and pin-
     " ches,
" Be dying for years—he fhould perifh by inches !
" And when from his body his fpirit fhall fever,
" He ought to be damn'd to damnation for ever ! ! !"

Such horrors prefented themfelves to his view,
That Sherry took fright at the picture he drew ;
He had fomething, 'twas thought, ftill more horrid to
     fay,
When his tongue loft its power, and he fainted away.
Some fay, 'twas his Confcience that gave him a ftrol
But thofe who beft know him, treat that as a joke ;

'Tis

'Tis a trick, which *Stage Orators* ufe in their need,
The Paffions to raife, and the Judgment miflead.——
When. FRANCIS beheld his friend SHERIDAN drop,
He fprung twenty feet at two fteps and a hop;
Affafœtida Drops, he applied to the nofe
Of his friend, who recovered his ftrength, and arofe—
But THURLOW, long filent, now thought it his turn
To fpeak to the Court, fo he moved to ADJOURN.

Yours, &c.

LETTER

LETTER II.

FROM

SIMPKIN THE SECOND

TO HIS

DEAR BROTHER IN WALES.

DEAR BROTHER,

——YOU aſk, why was FR——s diſtreſt?
Why he fear'd for the Cauſe ſo much more than the reſt?
To anſwer this queſtion as well I can,
I muſt give you a Sketch of this wonderful Man:

Some certain things riſe from the dark,
Our HERO ſtarted firſt a Clerk——
In Office, that was ſtill Impreſſing
On tender youth this uſeful Leſſon;

Thoſe

Thofe that would thrive, muſt learn to cringe,
" *To turn like door upon a hinge;*"
To flatter thofe that favour ſhew ye;
To ſpurn at thofe that are below ye;
FR——s by acting well this part,
Completely won his Patron's heart;
Who made him, by a ſudden ſpring,
The FIFTH PART *of a Potent King;* *
That is, he was to Bengal ſent,
The *under limb* of Government.——
Let yonder Beggar mount a Horfe,
The Proverb tells " which way his courfe;"
So FR——s, who had been a Hack
Of Office, 'midſt a fervile Pack,
Saw thouſands tremble at his nod,
And like another PHILIP'*s Son,* became a God.
Great his wealth had been indeed,
If HASTINGS had not check'd his ſpeed,
And to his profpects put an end,
By calling from LUCKNOW *his Friend.*
This FR——s never can forgive,
As long as he and HASTINGS live;
And from that time has been purfuing
Means to effect his total ruin;

* FRANCIS's definition of himſelf, and his Power, to the People in India.

But

But fruitless finding Opposition,
He form'd—*like some*—a Coalition:
But Coalitions still must fall,
One certain fate o'ertakes them all.
Tho' his—a novel kind of plan——
To join, and then betray the Man;
But Hastings' *Genius* was awake,
And ere he stung, it scorch'd the *Snake*.
This to the fire but added fuel,
Until it ended in a Duel.——
When Fr——s saw his schemes all fail,
For England's shore he spread his sail.——

No sooner on shore had our Phill set his feet,
Than he drove, like a *Post-boy*, to Leadenhall-street;
In the flames of his Malice, he burnt to disclose
A Tale, which had cost him some years to compose;
But he got a rebuff from the Court of Directors;
They were Hastings's Friends; they were *Virtue*'s
    Protectors;
They paid just regard to their Honor and Glory;
They read not Phill's Papers; they heard not Phill's
    Story.
Tho' like Light'ning to England from India he came,
In speed he was greatly surpass'd by his Fame;

They

They knew how the meafures of HASTINGS he croft,
How near his advice COROMANDEL had loft;
By the Court of Directors, it clearly was feen,
That the Man was a compound of Envy and Spleen—

Then away to the *Mongers of Boroughs* went he,
To try, if with fome one he could not agree ;
And find a fit corner—for once—to his ufe,
For *fpeech unreftrain'd*, and for *licens'd abufe.*

But when he found out each abufive Oration
Could produce no effect on a fenfible Nation,
His attention was turn'd to the *Quixote-like* BURKE,
Who is fond of engaging in Quixote-like Work;
He told him long Stories " of Damfels diftrefs'd,"
" Of extirpated Nations, of RAJAHS opprefs'd;"
Of HASTINGS's having compell'd the NABOB,
His *Kindred*, his *Mother*, *Grandmother*, to rob.——
Shall the eloquent BURKE, who by pleading the caufe,
Of *Powell* and *Bembridge*, gain'd lafting applaufe;
Shall the Man, who to Wretches like thefe was a friend,
The Rights of Old Damfels refufe to defend ?
Oh! let not the *Children of* ASIA befeech
Thy mercy in vain ; but the Tyrant *Impeach ;*
I myfelf will find *Matter*, do thou *furnifh Speech.*

Then

Then away posted BURKE to his CHARLEY and SHERRY,
Who were toping at BROOKES's, pot-valiant and merry!
" I have something, my BOYS, upon which we may
    prate,
'Tis time we should *Spout*, left we grow *out of date;*
Againft a NABOB I am furnifh'd with matter——
When matter is found, we can all of us chatter;
WARREN HASTINGS is he, you remember, his friends
Difappointed us lately, in gaining our ends.
That Stock-holding-Crew, the late change brought about
In Adminiftration, and turn'd us all out:
Let us try, in our turn, if we can't over-reach him,
Then HILLOA, *Brave Boys,* let us on and Impeach
    him!
Perhaps the rich Rogue, when he finds himfelf under
Our lafh, may prefent us fome part of the Plunder.
Then CHARLEY, who found himfelf not in a cue,
So wild, fo romantic a fcheme to purfue;
Who found by a Balance, juft made of his Books,
Himfelf better paid, by attending at BROOKES';
Requefted, that BURKE would be pleas'd to defift
From the bufinefs, or ftrike his Name out of the Lift.
And SHERRY, who now holds Theatrical Stuff,
Declar'd on the Stage, " there was *acting* enough."
And begg'd, that if BURKE had this Farce at his heart,
He might be prevented from playing a part.

BURKE

BURKE ſtarted, and ſwore, if you do not think fit
To ſupport me in this, *I'll go over to* PITT.
Then Charles, who began to foreſee the reduction
Of his force at *St. Stephen's*, might prove his deſtruc-
   tion;
Engag'd for himſelf, and the whole of his Party;
Tho' ſome people think CHARLES is not very hearty.
Three years have elaps'd ſince the ſuit they began,
They may work many more, let them do all they can,
Before they will conquer this *much-injur'd Man!*
You aſk'd me, what cauſe had the Houſe to reſiſt
Adding FR————s's name to the Managers' Liſt?
Why, all moderate men to exclude him agreed,
Tho' BURKE pledg'd his honour, he could not proceed
Without F————'s aid, to ſupport him in need.
Then, EDMUND! thy zeal ſtruck the guard from thy
   tongue,
And betray'd the baſe ſource, whence thy Charges all
   ſprung,
Great part of the Houſe, which till then had believ'd
Thy ſtory, now find themſelves groſsly deceiv'd;
How many good men, now are griev'd to the heart,
To think they were talk'd into taking a part.

But F————s triumphantly laughs in his ſleeve,
To think he ſo long could the public deceive.

C   As

As he walk'd along Bond-ftreet, he faid to a Friend,
" Tho' my Foe be acquitted, 'twill anfwer my end;
" Oppreft with fatigue, and o'er-burthen'd with coft,
" His health will be broken, his fortune be loft;"
Then he fwore, by the Lord, he would not ceafe pur-
    fuing,
Till Death and Damnation had finifh'd his ruin.
Tho' fo generous an Oath, he confefs'd, gave him pain,
To come from a bofom fo kind and humane.

   I conclude for the prefent :—but if, my dear Brother,
You like this Epiftle, I'll fend you another;
And ground there will be, quite enough, to your forrow,
For SHERRY begins his Oration To-morrow—
And *Sums up* the whole of the Charge as he goes :— ⎫
Tho' amidft all " this fumming,"—juft under the ⎬
    Rofe— ⎭
'Tis furprizing, he never fums up—*what he owes !*

               Yours, *&c.*

LETTER

LETTER III.

FROM

SIMPKIN THE SECOND

TO HIS

DEAR BROTHER IN WALES.

THE IMPEACHMENT.

YOU ASSURE me, *Dear Brother*, the comical Tales
I've related, amufe our *Acquaintance* in WALES ;
You beg me, as SHERRY proceeds to Impeach,
To give you in Rhime the *Contents of his Speech.*
The Tafk is too hard—for the Speech is fo fine,
It efcapes fuch a dull underftanding as mine.
Howe'er to oblige you as far as I can,
I'll begin an Oration as SHERRY began.

When

When the LORDS were affembled, and fet in their Places,
He rofe up, *brim-full of Theatrical Graces* :—

" Permit me, my LORDS, ere I fpeak more at large,

" To difclaim every Motive for making this Charge.

" Has the NABOB complain'd ? Is the Prifoner Accus'd

" At the fuit of thofe Ladies WE fay he Abus'd ?

" 'Tis the Caufe of Mankind, led by EDMUND the brave,

" His object is MAN, from *Man's Bafenefs* to fave.

" The MINISTER PITT, fays " the Treafury is drain'd;"

" But all muft admit they are much entertain'd.

" However, I'd have it be well underftood,

" If we have any Motive, 'tis certainly good.

" My LORDS, you expect Proofs conclufive and ftrong;

" But in that expectation, your Lordfhips are wrong :

" From documents written, no proof can we draw,

" Nor can *any one* fwear—to what *nobody faw.*

" I'm not pleading excufe for our failing in Proof,

. " For tho' we bring none, we can make out enough;

" I fhall make out enough from the Pris'ner's Defence,

" By giving *my* Meaning, and taking *his* Senfe.

" 'Tis faid, when the Houfe *a Delinquent Impeaches,*

" The MANAGERS fhould be correct in their Speeches :

" That is, they fhould make a plain fimple Narration

" Of Facts, well attefted, without aggravation :

" That *Legal Chicanery* fhould not affift

" To give the *Plain Senfe* an *Ingenious Twift.*

" But,

" But, *my* Lords, by your leave, the diftinction I'll trace,

" Betwixt *Mifdemeanor* and *Capital Cafe;*

" For unlefs we were certain your LORDSHIPS would
  " Hang him,

" The MANAGERS' Tongues claim a Licence to Bang
  " him.

" The PRISONER, my LORDS, under various pretences,

" Has fet up at times a long ftring of Defences:

" My LORDS, there *was one* to the COMMONS *addrefs'd,*

" But that to *your Lordfhips* is reckoned *the beft.*

" It feems that the former was *haftily* penn'd

" By thofe that would do it—*Acquaintance* or *Friend:*

" And as all common Men are but commonly wife,

" For the COMMONS, a *common Defence* would fuffice—

" And finding our Charges divided and fplit,

" Each *Journeyman* took what the MASTER thought
  " fit.

" My *fkill in finance*, Mr. SHORE, is your Lot:

" My *Confiftence* to prove, I rely upon SCOTT,

" And on MIDDLETON's *Memory*, when I've forgot.

" He thought, as the COMMONS themfelves were de-
  " puted,

" Our Party, by *Deputy*, might be confuted;

" But now that your LORDSHIPS have call'd him before
  " ye,

" At your Bar it behoves him to tell his own Story,

" But

" But, my LORDS, we object to this shifting of ground—

" For the Conduct of Journeymen, Masters are bound.

" Would it not be, my LORDS, most surprising and
    " strange,

" If EDMUND OUR CHIEF, *his opinion should change?*

" If having persuaded the COMMONS to join

" In the Vote, he should take up a different Line,

" And say, " *The Impeachment was* YOURS, and *not*
    " MINE :"

" That he ever was HASTINGS's *friend* in his Heart,

" Tho' compell'd to accept of a MANAGER's Part?"

While SHERRY was speaking, I could not conceive

Why the Lords and the Commons all laugh'd in their
    Sleeve;

Why BURKE fear'd that SHERRY was out of his
    Track,

Why FOX's sweet face look'd a little more black—

But since I have learnt, that the Picture he drew,

Was the *likeness of something* that most people knew—

That BURKE and CHARLES FOX had conjointly brought
    forth

The very same Arguments—*versus*—LORD NORTH.

That CHARLES would not " trust his dear person a Mi-
    nute"

Alone with LORD NORTH, so much danger was in it.

And

And BURKE, with *Impeachments* the Houfe to fupply,
Carry'd fome in his Pocket, " cut ready and dry."
I am told, it has long been his cuftom to take 'em
Wherever he goes, like a Prieft's " Vade Mecum."
St. STEPHEN's refounded with SCAFFOLD and BLOCK,
NORTH fell from the Treafury Bench with a fhock.
" Throw a Bone to a Dog, and no longer he fnarls,"
So NORTH threw a Bone out to EDMUND and CHAR-
    LES;
That is, they determined, if PITT had not feen 'em,
To fhare all the *Loaves and the Fifhes* between 'em.
From that moment have CHARLEY and EDMUND agreed
That NORTH muft be honeft and noble indeed!
BURKE fearches for elegant Phrafe to commend :—
And CHARLES too is happy to call him his Friend.

As SHERRY in fpeaking is fond of Precifion,
He adopts the *Theatrical mode of Divifion* :——
That is, he arranges the *Plot* and the *Facts*,
And the Play will confift of a *Number of Acts*.
ONE ACT was gone through when the Poft-bell was
    ringing,
Which unluckily puts a full ftop to my finging,
Howe'er, if this Letter can add to your pleafure,
I'll fend you another as foon as I've leifure.

LETTER

L E T T E R IV.

F R O M

SIMPKIN THE SECOND

T O H I S

DEAR BROTHER IN WALES.

AGAIN, *my dear Brother*, I take up the Quill,
My Debt to *difcharge*, and my promife fulfil.
Thus SHERRY began :—" Now, my Lords, I proceed
" Some loofe and confus'd Affidavits to read:
" I'll allow to be true every word they contain;
" But permit me their Meaning and Senfe to explain.
" My Lords, there was fwearing by Foot and Dragoons;
" By *Vollies* fome fwore, and fome fwore by *Platoons ;*
" Thefe Swearings, I call Sir ELIJAH's *Collection,*
" Intended to prove a well known Infurrection:

" But,

" But, my Lords, you fhall prefently fee me victori-
" ous

" Over this Infurrection, however notorious;

" After what I have faid, will the *Counfel* infift

" That any Rebellion did ever exift?

" This point being fettled:—I now take my courfe

" To Asoph ul Dowlah's Attendants and Horfe;

" That he had 2000, the *Counfel* contended,

" But that's a pofition that can't be defended.

" My Lords, I infift that *Two Hundred*'s the moft;

" The reft had deferted, were jaded, or loft:

" Befides, I requeft it may not be forgot

" The rate Asoph travell'd, *full gallop* or *trot;*

" And 'twas right that the Nabob fhould travel *incog.*

" By poft or by *Doulb*, without Baggage or clog,

" To fupprefs, like himfelf, *a Rebellion incog.*

" But I'll give them Two Thoufand, with *Baryhoes* and
" *Coolies*,

" With Elephants, Camels, with *Hackrees* and *Doolies!*

" The *Counfel* fome proof have endeavoured to bring,

" That the Begums lent aid to the Rajah Cheyt
" Sing

" One Thoufand *Negecls*—but I boldly avow

" They were Fellows with *Matchlocks,* detach'd from
" Lucknow;

D   " But

" But where ever they came from, I care not about 'em,

" For your Lordſhips ſhall ſee, in five minutes I'll rou

    " 'em.

" SADUT ALLY, they ſay, in Conſpiracy join'd,

" And I aſk'd Sir ELIJAH, why HE was not fin'd?

" Sir ELIJAH, my Lords, gave a very good reaſon,

" The Man who is *Poor*, can't be *guilty of Treaſon*.

" His ſafety was then to *Inſolvency* due—

" *An Axiom, I find, inconteſtably true*

" My Lords, I ſhall prove this commotion and riſing

" Was not of my Ladies the BEGUMS' deviſing,

" And their *Eunuchs*, poor creatures, ſo gentle and

    " mild!

" Are unable to injure Man, Woman, or Child

" Colonel HANNAY himſelf, I can prove, was the Man

" From whoſe cruelties all the Diſturbance began:

" And this to eſtabliſh, *no Witneſs* I call,

" Save the elegant Letters of *Naylor* and *Hall*.

" The BEGUMS' Jaghire Major *Naylor* march'd thro,'

" 'Twixt the *Goomty* and *Gagra* his route to purſue;

" Where for ſome little time his Battalions were halted,

" Some RAJAH to quell, who, he ſays, had revolted.

" This Revolt, I preſume, muſt have been a miſtake,

" So I paſs over that, for his Memory's ſake.

" But when to the country of *Hannay* he came,

" He found nothing elſe but combuſtion and flame.

                    " The

" The Army of Rebels the *Major* o'erthrew;
" He frighted their Heroes;—he wounded and flew.
" Thefe poor dying Wretches, that made no refiftance.
" He offer'd to cure:—They refus'd his affiftance.
" The *Counfel* may fay, 'tis from prejudice ftrong,
".Thofe Men their exiftence refus'd to prolong;
" That a *Foreigner's touch* would a BRAMIN pollute;
" But Prejudice *now* 'tis my turn to difpute.
" Thefe Folks were from fuch foolifh prejudice free—
" They were Patriots, my Lords, of the higheft degree:
" They died that their blood to *their* GODS *might afcend*,
" Who till now to their cries had not time to attend!"

Four hours and an half, ere he came to a clofe,
Did SHERRY declaim on fuch topics as thofe:
He ended at length, with a Compliment fine
To BURKE, whom he ftiled, " fomething more than
  divine!"
For giving himfelf this occafion to fhine.
And BURKE, to whom nothing's more odious and hate-
  ful,
Than the Man who for favour conferr'd is ungrateful,
Opportunity found, with *large Int'reft* to pay
The Compliments back, on the very fame day.
One Man had, it feems, the prefumption to ftate,
The IMPEACHMENT *Expence* was enormoufly great:

When

When BURKE, in a moment, fprung up in his place,
And cry'd, as he ftar'd the Man full in the face, }
" Such ftinginefs, Sir, would a Nation difgrace!
" After all the fine things we've heard SHERIDAN fay,
" He's a pitiful Wretch who refufes to pay:
" Now that Genius has blinded our Eyes with its flafh,
" Can we look on Accounts? Can we fum up our Cafh?
" After foaring above all the Regions of Senfe,
" Can we tumble fo low as to think about Pence?
" Has not SHERRY, this morning, expos'd to your view,
" All the beauties of Thefpis, and Cicero too?
" To the BISHOPS, he gave an example of Preaching,
" To the COMMONS, a model of future Impeaching;
" HISTORIANS, hereafter, fhall copy his Diction,
" And POETS themfelves may learn Leffons of Fiction;
" RHETORICIANS are taught the arrangements of
        " Flowers,
" To the Bufkin and Sock he has given new powers:
" The PAINTERS may learn finer Pictures to draw,
" And the JUDGES new Modes of interpreting Law.
" From him may the ORATOR learn to prevail,
" Ly Action and Sound, when his Arguments fail:
" The PHILOSOPHER too, may learn nature to fift;
" The Attorney, to cloak a bad Caufe with a Shift.
" Now fince every profeffion fome benefit draws
" I can't think for a moment of ftarving the Caufe!"

No fooner was EDMUND fat down, than a *Spark*
Arofe in his place, and beg'd leave to remark,
" That himfelf and fome others remember'd the day,
" When the MAN *who fo freely votes Thoufands away,*
" For hearing a Speech, or for feeing a Play,
" Was once in His MAJESTY's *Kitchen* fo fparing,
" As to *limit the Cheefe,* nay, to *hufband the paring!*"

And now, *my dear Bróther,* I lay down my Pen,
Which after next Tuefday I'll take up again.

LETTER

LETTER V.

FROM

SIMPKIN THE SECOND

TO HIS

DEAR BROTHER IN WALES.

MR. SHERIDAN.—THE THIRD DAY.

DEAR BROTHER,

WERE it not that I fear you would deem it neglect,
Or accuse me, perhaps, of the *want of respect*;
I would pass o'er in silence the Speech of this day;
For SIMPKIN, like SHERRY, wants something to say.
The PEERESSES thought there would rise a *new Sun,*
And that former out-doings, would now be out-done!

At

At *Six* in the morning, 'tis faid they arofe—
By *Eight* drefs'd their heads, by *Nine* put on their
    clothes—
By *Ten* took their places in high expectation,
Of feeing this SHERIDAN *Act an Oration.*
By *half after Twelve*, or at fartheft by *One*,
The PEERS were affembled—the PLAY was begun.
Two hours he harangued, but I little remember,
" Save IMPEY and DAVY, and 12*th of December.*"
He defcrib'd a circuitous ftring of Suggeftions,
And put to *the Counfel* fome very clofe Queftions.
He knew he might fafely their anfwers defy,
Since the forms of the COURT *would not let them reply.*
As the Senfe of his Speech was but ill underftood
By myfelf, I conclude 'twas uncommonly good.
When his Genius inflammable rofe to its height,
Like LUNARDI's *Balloon*, it efcap'd from our fight:
And as when fome Balloon at its equipoife pitch,
Lofes part of its air by the *break of a ftitch*,
The *high-flying* HERO no remedy knows,
And the Car tumbles down with more fpeed than it
    rofe:
So the high-flying SHERRY difcover'd at length,
That Orators may foar too high for their ftrength.
For juft as his voice was rais'd up to its top,
The Court, with furprize, faw him fuddenly ftop.

                                        Then

Then ADAM ftep'd forward, and faid " *that his friend,*
" *Was feiz'd with a—a—trifling—and therefore muft end.*"
This accident, Brother, muft greatly diminifh.
The length of my Letter; and here I fhould finifh,
Were it not that I heard fome *odd jocular Sparks*
Converfing together, and making remarks.
A *Trifling!* faid one, as he laugh'd very hearty,
Has long been the common *Difeafe of the Party.*
LORD ———, who is one of your old fafhion'd Peers,
That wants to find MEANING *in all that he hears,*
Said, " that our Orators *now,* were not fram'd to his
" tafte,
" They carry no *weight,* they're conftructed in hafte;
" And like our *Mail Coaches,* that travel fo faft,
" Muft now and then get an unfortunate caft."
One Gentleman faid, " where he reafons on facts,
" We find SHERRY dull; but whenever *he acts,*
" In five minutes time he difplays to our view,
" The *Tragic,* the *Comic,* the *Pantomime* too:"
He added, that all the Great Men of our Nation,
Would adopt a new Plan for their Sons' Education;
They find it now ufelefs to lay in a ftock
Of Logic, by reading *fuch Authors as* LOCKE;
They find *graceful Action* and *elegant Diction,*
More powerful than Reafon to carry Conviction:
So a new fet of Tutors they mean to engage—
The very beft Actors they find on the Stage;

Some

Some *Mafter*, like SIDDONS, whofe Pathos excels—
Or whofe Leffons fhall imitate *Nature* like WELLS.
And the Lawyers, it feems, who attend the King's
    Courts,
No longer will trouble themfelves with Reports.
The Student finds COKE *upon* LYTTLETON, dry,
And with *Johnfon* and *Shakefpeare* his place will fupply;
In fhort, the *Old* ORATOR's * anfwer is true—
" That *Aaion*, and *nothing but* ACTION, will do !"
Here then I conclude, and fhall filent remain,
Till SHERRY begins his Oration again.

---

  * Alluding to the Philofopher, who being afked what was the
firft qualification of an Orator, anfwered, *Aaion*; what the fecond, *Aaion*; what the third, *Aaion*; meaning thereby, that
Aaion was enough for an Orator.

LETTER VI.

FROM

SIMPKIN THE SECOND

TO HIS

DEAR BROTHER IN WALES.

MR. SHERIDAN.—THE FOURTH DAY.

DEAR BROTHER, at laſt I've the Pleaſure to ſay,
That the Orator cloſ'd his Oration this day.
Tho' EDMUND *his Chief,* who ſuppoſes the ſtrength
And effect of a ſpeech correſpond with its length,
In a whiſper obſerv'd—" Now you may find yourſelf
    ſtronger,
" You might as well ſpeak for a *week or two longer*."

Thus

Thus SHERRY began:—" Much indebted I own
" Myſelf to this COURT, for the favour they've ſhewn;
" My LORDS, you'll excuſe my again going o'er
" The ground I have travers'd ſo often before;
" Your Lordſhips remember I left oft with reading
" The *Narrative Part*—and I now am proceeding
" To bring from behind the thick miſt of Confuſion
" A *fraudulent Friendſhip*, and *friendly Colluſion*.
" Theſe things came to light from the reading a
  " Letter—
" A *private Epiſtle*, and ſo much the better—
" When in private and public we find contradiction,
" That Letter which tends to the *Priſoner's conviction*—
" That Letter alone we bring forward to view—
" Convinc'd that none elſe can be poſſibly true.
" The Priſoner, it ſeems, thought it matter of wonder
" That MIDDLETON gave him no part of the Plunder;
" That the diff'rence 'twixt him and his Agent was
  " wider   •
" Than that between LION and *Lion's Provider;*
" That at leaſt it became an *obedient Jackal*
" To remember the *Lion*, and not ſwallow all.
" My Lord, tho' we make out no *poſitive Proof*
" That theſe were his thoughts, we've ſuſpicion enough;
" And I truſt that this Court will give ready admiſſion,
" In *failure of Proofs*, to ASSERTED SUSPICION.

" My Lords, there have been many Letters fuppreft,

" Some made for the purpofe, and fome better dreft.

" There was one from the NABOB, by which it
    " appears

" He wifh'd not to take the Bow BEGUM's *Jaghires.*

" Thefe PRINCESSES had (what our Ladies would
    " think'

" Not uncommon) a *whim for good victuals and drink—*

" Too long in the habit of cutting and carving,

" To relifh the Fafhion of pinching and ftarving.

" Now the Prifoner, who wickedly wanted to force

" Thofe Ladies to follow fome defperate courfe,

" Thought nothing fo likely to ftir up a riot,

" As to *weaken their Tea,* or to *alter their Diet.*

" Not all the tyrannical acts of paft Ages,

" Not TACITUS; *No!* not the luminous Pages

" Of GIBON *himfelf,* can an inftance produce

" Of Authority turn'd to fo wicked a ufe ;

" No fuch cruelty ever was exercifed in

" This World, fince the days of ORIGINAL SIN !

" As to force an affectionate dutiful Son

" To act by *his Mother as* ASOPH has done.

" He forgot in our SHAKESPEARE that precept
    " Divine,

" *Let thy Mind be untainted, and nothing defign*

" Againft

" *Againſt thy Dear Mother!*" No, this he forgot——

" Or if he remember'd, he minded it not.

" 'Twas hoped that the BEGUMS would openly riſe,

" And aſſemble a Hoſt by the Sound of their cries;

" That HASTINGS might find ſome excuſe for the
  " meaſure

" He meant to adopt with reſpect to their Treaſure.

" But the BEGUMS, my Lords, tho' of millions bereft,

" *Could live pretty well upon that which was left:*

" They are ſtricken in years, they are gentle and meek;

" No reſentment they feel, and no vengeance they ſeek.

" E'en now that ourſelves with ſuch zeal are purſuing

" This Man, THEY *would weep* if they heard of his
  " ruin.

" 'Twas expedient, my Lords, that theſe Dames ſhou'd
  " rebel,

" Or be thought ſo at leaſt, which would anſwer as well.

" So IMPEY ſet off, and collected a pack

" Of ſtrange *Affidavits*, ſome white and ſome black,

" And return'd with a budget brim full in a crack.

" One day, the CHIEF JUSTICE was travelling poſt—

" The next at LUCKNOW, when, like *Old* HAMLET's
  " *Ghoſt,*

" *Swear! Swear!* you muſt *Swear!* was *Old* TRUE-
  " PENNY's cry,

" To thoſe who ſtood near, and to thoſe that paſs'd by."

" My

" My Lords, this great Man, in affeffing the rate
" Of Crimes, had an eye to the wants of the State:
" Justinian and Timur he treated as fools,
" And was guided by Cocker's *Numerical Rules.*
" *Ye* Guardians *of Juſtice,* to you I appeal—
" Shall *Private* give way to the *General Weal?*
" *Ye* Prelates, to whom our Religion belongs,
" Our Country to fave may we do private wrongs?
" To decide on this Queſtion, my Lords, is your lot,
" Whether Hastings's conduct was ufeful or not?
" Let the Truth *but* appear, and the Battle is won,
" The Verdict is ours!—Now, my Lords, *I have*
   " *done!*"

The *Gallery folk,* who, mifled by the fport,
Conceived 'twas a *Play-Houſe inſtead of a* Court;
And thinking the Actor uncommonly good,
They Clap'd, and cry'd " Bravo!" as loud as they
   could.
Then Edmund gave Sherry a hearty embrace,
And cry'd, as he fputter'd all over his face,
" *At Supper this night thou ſhalt have the* First
   " Place!"
On thy Leader's right hand be thy dignify'd feat;
Fat Beef and fat Mutton fhall garnifh thy Plate;

And when thou haſt ſupp'd, to enliven the ſoul,
Shall Claret and Burgundy fill up thy Bowl!
The HEROES, who long and ſuccefsfully fight,
From the *Edicts of* HOMER eſtabliſh a right
To enjoy the rich Feaſt with BRISEIS at night.

And now, till the Court ſhall think fit to renew
The Trial, *Dear* BROTHER, I bid you adieu.

LETTER

TO

. SIMPKIN THE SECOND IN LONDON.

FORGIVE me, *Dear Sim*, if I'm not deeply ſmitten,
With your half dozen Letters ſo fluently written;
And ſince, after SHERIDAN's heart-ſtirring ſummons,
A pauſe is judg'd *prudent* by LORDS as by COMMONS;
And leiſure may leave you to liſten inclin'd,
I embrace a fit moment to tell you my mind.

Methinks, *Brother Sim*, your adventure was bold,
When you ſtep'd forth an ape of *your Nameſake of old :*
That Simpkin ſo pleaſant, whoſe well-mingled ſatire,
Ow'd no poiſon to Party, no gall to ill-nature;
From Talents and Virtue withholding his ſneer,
At Folly He laugh'd, and the laugh was *ſincere :*
In Vanity's Vortex his models he choſe,
And *Coxcombs*, and *Pedants* alone were his foes.

But you, *my Dear Brother*, with feelings more nice,
Find ridicule lurking in——horror of Vice;

And

And efforts of Genius acute and refin'd,
That honour our Country, our Age and Mankind,
Deform'd in your Verfe, take a farcical mein,
Where Pleafantry check'd, wears the features of Spleen:
Too angry for Humour, for Cenfure too gay,
Your Irony dies in plain ftory away.
And, while we lament that your Arrows are fhot,
Where Envy and Party in vain feek a blot,
We cannot avoid, *Brother Simpkin*, be fure,
Sufpecting your motives may not be quite pure.
And thus, when you tell us you're glad to the heart,
" *That the ORATOR SHERRY *has finifh'd his part;*"
When you fay " *that fome Letters are meant for* CON-
    " VICTION,"
We own that you there drop the *language of Fiction.*
Beware, *Brother Simpkin*, this Painter fublime,
Who has lately engrofs'd your befpattering Rhyme,
In a playful effufion of Fancy has fhewn,
A PORTRAIT that fome may miftake for *your own*;
A *Plagiary Author*, Retailer of Scraps,
Purloin'd from a Brother—from ANSTEY perhaps:
All Candour without, but all Envy within,
A Smile ill concealing the horrible grin;

---

* Vide Simpkin's 6th Letter.

Who

Who fain would be witty and archly fevere,
While from eyes fwoln with rage, gufhes forth the
    hot tear.
The *Picture in* PARSONS yet gladdens the fcene,
Nor need I repeat, 'tis SIR FRETFUL I mean.

  Then warn'd, *My Dear Brother*, with SHERRY
    have done,
Nor hang up your Blanket 'twixt us and the Sun;
For lo! through the pores of your thread-bare defign,
They rays of the God more refplendently fhine.

SIMPKIN

NOTICING SIMON.

SOME fellow, *Dear Brother*, affuming your Name,
My Letters to you has thought proper to blame;
His Cenfure's convey'd in a diffonant Chime,
With *one Line for Senfe*, and *another for Rhyme!*
He talks about, " SHERIDAN's Heart-ftirring Summons"
For no other ufe but to *jingle* with *Commons;*
Then he fpeaks of " *Old* SIMPKIN, whofe well-min-
  glad fatire
" Ow'd no Poifon to Party, no Gall to Ill-nature."
Such uncouth ideas in every line
Prove clearly, the Writer's *no Brother of mine.*
He tells me, forfooth, " that he's not deeply fmitten
" With my half dozen Letters fo fluently written :"
Were he not below notice, fome Lines I would write
  him,
That, if he can feel, fhould effectually fmite him.
One moment *he thinks,* and the next *he is fure,*
That " my motive for writting is not very pure."
If SIMPKIN *the Second* he really knew,
He would own, with a blufh, his *Sufpicion untrue.*

By his boldly obtruding *Suspicion* for KNOWLEDGE,
One would think him a *Student of* SHERIDAN's *College*;
But when I confider how feeble his Pen,
SHERRY never could own him—*as one of his Men.*
Once more then, *Dear Brother*, I bid you adieu,
And will write nothing more till *requested by you.*

P. S.—As to SHERRY himfelf—juft to fill up the void,
In fuppreffing all Theatres, now he's employ'd;
And having in ACTING accomplifh'd fome Fame,
He's preventing all others—from doing the fame.
For that excellent Maxim has ne'er met his eye,
" *Do to others, good Man, as you would be done by.*"

THE

REAL SIMON IN WALES

TO

SIMPKIN THE SECOND IN LONDON.

My Y *dear Brother* SIMPKIN, with heartfelt concern,
From reading *The* WORLD *of laſt Monday*, I learn,
That ſome impudent Knave had the boldneſs to ſend you
Some Lines *in my Name*, with a view to offend you.
The Work I diſclaim, and 'tis my reſolution,
If I find out the Rogue, to commence Proſecution.
No, BROTHER, your Letters muſt always delight us,
And we hope you will ever continue to write us.
When the *Simpleton* call'd you " Retailer of Scraps,"
One would think that he meant to give SHERIDAN
        Slaps:
Of Novelty careleſs, *you* only profeſs
To give SHERIDAN'S *Speech* a *Poetical Dreſs.*

                                        Sir

3862

Sir LAWRENCE LLEWELLYN, return'd to his Seat,
Laſt night gave his Friends, the Electors, a Treat;
Sir LAWRENCE, you know, is a Man of high breeding,
And exceſſively fond of *Theatrical Reading;*
He ſaid, "SHERRY'*s Speech* was an excellent Piece
" Of *Patch Work,* with Shreds brought from ROME and
  from GREECE;
" But ſhould Poets and Orators try him for Theft—
" Like the *Jackdaw* of old, would a Feather be left?"
Sir LAWRENCE obſerv'd, 'twas exceedingly odd,
To hear of an Actor becoming a God.
But he thinks this *new* GOD, ſhould in gratitude foſter
And ſupport his Creator—this SIMON *Impoſtor.*
Sir LAWRENCE conſider'd the Scribbler's obtruſion
Of Sir FRETFUL, a very unhappy alluſion.
Now, I bid you farewell, till the PARLIAMENT ends,
When, I hope *My Dear* SIMPKIN will viſit his Friends.

F I N I S.

www.ingramcontent.com/pod-product-compliance
Lightning Source LLC
Chambersburg PA
CBHW022204020726
47496CB00008B/2869